cool chicago

an inspirational guide to what's best in the city

Kathleen Maguire is a lifelong resident of Chicago and author of the bestselling book *Chicago Then and Now*. As a tour guide for Walk Chicago Tours, she brings Chicago's brilliance and magic firsthand to its visitors. Kathleen currently lives in Chicago's Lincoln Square.

Kathleen would like to thank Chicago's visitors for their interest and enthusiasm and, as always and most of all, Terry Sullivan for his unending support and inspiring storytelling.

The publishers would like to thank photographer Karl Mondon for all of the specially commissioned pictures in this book.

First published in the United Kingdom in 2014 by
PAVILION BOOKS
an imprint of Pavilion Books Company Ltd.
1 Gower Street, London WC1E 6HD, UK

ISBN: 978-1-90981-5612

A CIP catalogue record for this book is available from the British Library.

10 9 8 7 6 5 4 3 2 1

Repro by Mission Productions Ltd, Hong Kong
Printed by Times Offset (M) Sdn Bhd, Malaysia

cool chicago

an inspirational guide to what's best in the city

Kathleen Maguire

PAVILION

Introduction

I've never met anyone who doesn't think Chicago is cool, whether a longtime resident or an occasional visitor – no matter what decade or which time of year. From its most current attractions to its most dynamic neighborhoods, the city retains an unflappable sense of "cool" – Chicago will never go out of style.

This is not to say that certain sites and neighborhoods aren't "trending" at any particular time. Like anywhere else, in Chicago what is fashionable can come and go quickly – sometimes because of its very popularity. When something becomes too well-known, it can lose the edginess that made it a great fit for Chicago in the first place. The rents go up and the chains move in, and suddenly what was edgy is no longer so, as anyone who drank coffee in Wicker Park or rented a loft in Pilsen has witnessed firsthand.

But "cool" doesn't come and go. Or, it goes before it becomes decidedly uncool. Take Hot Doug's, for example. This out-of-the-way sausage shop with its lines around the block – when you could find it open – was slotted for this book. The place that offered free food for life to anyone sporting a Hot Doug's tattoo closed in 2014, after its owner decided, "It's time to do something else." This might make Hot Doug's very uncool for anyone with one of those tattoos, but the whimsical quality of its story reflects the character of a city that will always be on the edge.

And perhaps this whimsical story is a cautionary tale for the reading of this book. Entries were carefully chosen for their combined qualities of edginess and endurance, like Chicago itself. Arranged from the lakefront outward, sites in *Cool Chicago* range from art and architecture to fast food, from theaters to taverns, from bookshops to breweries, all distinctive to Chicago, and all independent – or at least begun that way. Garrett's Popcorn (see page 52), for example, while now an international corporation, is still required Chicago eating for visitors and residents alike. Even a tourist hot spot like the Skydeck (see page 36) epitomizes cool and edgy in a very literal way. And whether it's below freezing or warm enough for shorts on the day of the St. Patrick's Day parade, there may be no cooler moment in the city than the day every year when the river turns green (see page 46).

In full disclosure, I've only been to the Skydeck for professional reasons. But many Chicagoans have been to the Sears (now Willis) Tower's observation deck, which was the cool thing before architects pushed the edges – in this case a little more than four feet beyond the building's footprint. I can't think of anything cooler than witnessing what seems ordinary in the most extraordinary ways, floating in a glass box 1,353 feet above the Loop or peering into the funhouse version of an iconic skyline through *Cloud Gate* (see page 6). Chicago is a city that offers these new ways of seeing, occasionally fashionable but unstoppably cool.

Said to have been inspired by liquid mercury, British sculptor Anish Kapoor's inspirational design was chosen over work by 30 different artists. The surface of the sculpture, nicknamed "The Bean" reflects and distorts the city's skyline. Visitors are able to walk around and under *Cloud Gate*'s 12-foot-high arch. On the underside is the "omphalos" (Greek for "navel"), a concave chamber that warps and multiplies reflections. The sculpture builds upon many of Kapoor's artistic themes, and is popular with tourists as a photo-taking opportunity for its unique reflective properties. *Cloud Gate*'s closest rival was a 150-foot replica of a playground slide proposed by Jeff Koons. After Kapoor's design was chosen, numerous technological concerns regarding the design's construction and assembly arose, in addition to concerns regarding the sculpture's upkeep and maintenance. Various experts were consulted, some of whom believed the design could not be implemented. Eventually, a feasible method was found, but the sculpture's construction fell behind schedule. It was unveiled in an incomplete form during the Millennium Park grand opening celebration in 2004, before being concealed again while it was completed. *Cloud Gate* was formally dedicated on May 15, 2006, and has since gained considerable popularity, both domestically and internationally.

Architect Frank Gehry designed what many have labeled as Millennium Park's "showstopper." The Jay Pritzker Pavilion is a bandshell constructed between June 1999 and July 2004, opening officially on July 16, 2004. Since 1836 there have been height limitations on any building east of Michigan Avenue. To get around this, planners designated the pavilion as a "work of art." The pavilion, which has a capacity of 11,000, complements Petrillo Music Shell, Chicago's earlier and larger outdoor venue, located in adjacent Grant Park. Pritzker Pavilion is built partially atop the Harris Theater for Music and Dance, Millennium Park's indoor performing arts venue, with which it shares backstage facilities. Jay Pritzker Pavilion cost $60 million, a quarter of which came from the Pritzker family donation. It includes 4,000 fixed seats and a 95,000-square-foot Great Lawn that can accommodate an additional 7,000 people.

McCormick Tribune Ice Rink

Sweltering summers, frigid winters, and a lack of natural ponds pose no obstacle for Chicagoans who want to skate on ice. But even ice skating has a controversial political history in Chicago. The site of the McCormick Tribune Ice Rink, coveted lakefront property, was the subject of a long and complicated legal battle between private land developers and keepers of the public trust, finally ending up in the hands of the Illinois Central Railroad. At the time of Millennium Park's construction, the IC was no longer using the railyard where the McCormick Tribune Ice Rink now stands – free and open to the public. The rink was the first of Millennium Park's attractions to be opened to the public, in December 2001, and has been in operation every winter since. In the spirit of free public outdoor space, skaters can enjoy the rink from mid-November through early March, seven days a week, including most holidays. Skating lessons are also available for free on weekends, one hour before the rink opens. The only thing that will cost you is skate rental and the hot chocolate at Park Café.

Chicago has always welcomed – and even invited – radical artistic statements, and its public art is no exception. From its murals to its fine-art installations, public art in Chicago has always made a statement. *Crown Fountain*, named for the benefactors who paid for its installation, is a conception of Barcelona artist Jaume Plensa. True to the mission of public art, Plensa's creation reflects – literally and figuratively – a city that is constantly evolving in its culture and in its technology. The interactive "fountain" consists of two 50-foot blocks of steel-framed glass on either side of a reflecting pool. The glass blocks house LED screens behind a cascading film of water. The screens project the multicolored faces of Chicagoans who gaze out at visitors before releasing a spigot of water into the reflecting pool upon dozens of wading children of all sizes and colors. The magnificence of the fountain reflects – literally – not only the city's diversity but also its tendency to "make no little plans." Millennium Park's modern design departs from the classical style envisaged in Daniel Burnham's 1909 Plan of Chicago, but its scope is just as ambitious.

Harold Washington Social Security Center

The art at the Harold Washington Social Security Center injects some much-needed color and whimsy to a building which, from certain angles, resembles a prison. In fact, both Ilya Bolotowsky's mural and Claes Oldenburg's *Batcolumn* are part of the General Services Administration's Art in Architecture program, which commissions artwork to enliven federal buildings. Bolotowsky's "neoplastic" style complements the porcelainized steel he was asked to use for the piece, and its geometric arrangement of bold primary colors creates a sense of solidity as visitors enter the lobby. Oldenburg's *Batcolumn*, on the other hand, implies a certain irreverence toward the bold steel and concrete skyscrapers that surround it. The hollow, latticed steel allows the 100-foot baseball bat to withstand Chicago's winds, and leaves many wondering whether it is a monument to Chicago's innovative skyscraper design or the representation of a sport that illustrates the city's greatest rivalry. As with most of Chicago's public art, visitors can decide for themselves. Completed in 1976-77, these pieces followed the GSA's first Chicago project – Alexander Calder's 1974 *Flamingo*.

Chicago Cultural Center

78 E. Washington Street

When the Chicago Public Library's main branch was relocated to the new Harold Washington Library at State and Congress in 1991, this extraordinary building was saved from demolition by Eleanor Daley – widow of longtime Chicago mayor Richard J. Daley and mother of future mayor Richard M. Daley – who reinvented it as the Chicago Cultural Center. The center offers hundreds of free public events each year including tours, art exhibitions, concerts, and performance art. One of its biggest draws is the world's largest Tiffany stained-glass dome, with its 38-foot diameter and 30,000 pieces of glass, each of which was carefully cleaned and replaced in a 2009 restoration. The Chicago Cultural Center is a popular venue for weddings and other private events, proceeds from which are used to support the center's free public programs. For those on a tighter budget, $10 buys a couple a ceremony with a Justice of the Peace in GAR (Grand Army of the Republic) Hall, among its floor-to-ceiling windows and ornate ceiling architecture. Ceremonies are held one Saturday per month, by appointment only.

The Pedway includes about five miles of underground, street level, and above-ground walkways. It connects at least 40 buildings across the Loop, both public and private, and several public transit stations. The circular Pedway beneath the State of Illinois Center radiates north toward the Chicago River, east toward Millennium Park, and south toward the Loop. Pedestrians can travel from the State of Illinois Center all the way to the northeast and southwest corners of Millennium Park, stopping at Macy's along the way. The Pedway is also a former crime scene. Beneath the southwest corner of Randolph & Michigan, *Tribune* police reporter Jake Lingle was shot in the head on June 9, 1930. A known acquaintance of Al Capone – an important source for a crime reporter – maybe Lingle was talking too much to the wrong people, although evidence suggested an amicable relationship between the two. A man named Leo Brothers was convicted of the shooting, but he received a minimal sentence of 14 years, and served seven. The investigation never uncovered the reason that someone wanted Lingle killed, and Brothers took whatever he knew to his grave.

Marc Chagall designed the 4,000 square feet of mosaic that would become a permanent installation in Chicago's public art scene from his studio in France. Visiting the construction of the mural in Chicago in the summer of 1972, Chagall was pleased with what he saw, except for – as the story goes – the east panel. He decided he wanted more blue, as much blue as the west panel, as blue is the motif color to draw the eye of the viewer around all four sides. He came back in late summer to discover his orders had not been duly carried out – the lower right section of the panel was dominated by amber and gold in keeping with that panel's theme: summer. An angry Chagall began pounding away at the finished work, sending imported glass flying everywhere, and proceeded to haphazardly slap blue tile into cement. His finishing touches resulted in the amorphous blue blob that floats arbitrarily in front of the Hancock building. Chagall signed several corners of the mural, and at the dedication ceremony in 1974, he kissed Mayor Richard J. Daley on the cheek.

The Berghoff restaurant was opened in 1898 by Herman Joseph Berghoff and has become a Chicago landmark. Herman and his three brothers came to America from Dortmund, Germany, in 1870 and started brewing Berghoff's Beer in Fort Wayne, Indiana, in 1887. Herman wanted to expand the market for the family's beer and to do so he sold beer at the Chicago World's Fair of 1893. The popularity of the beer inspired Herman to open a café to showcase Berghoff's Dortmunder-style beer, which it sold for a nickel. Sandwiches were offered for free. The bar remained open even through the Prohibition era by selling a near beer (which is now sold as Berghoff's Root Beer) and Bergo Soda Pop and becoming a full-service restaurant. After Prohibition was repealed in 1933, the Berghoff was issued Liquor License No. 1. Long after most restaurants ended the practice, the Berghoff maintained a separate bar for men only. The segregation ended in 1969, when seven members of the National Organization for Women, including Gloria Steinem, sat at the bar and demanded service.

Alexander Calder was named an honorary citizen of Chicago on the day his iconic sculpture was dedicated, in a circus-like atmosphere like the one that inspired Calder's colorful, whimsical style of sculpture. On a sunny Friday afternoon in October 1974, the 76-year-old sculptor rode down State Street with Mayor Richard J. Daley atop a bandwagon pulled by 40 horses in a literal circus parade, replete with clowns, calliopes, and elephants. When they reached Federal Plaza, the two men used a five-foot cardboard pair of scissors to snip the ribbon around the sculpture, and the official dedication was marked by the release of hundreds of multicolored balloons into the sky. The balloons and the *Flamingo* sculpture created a dramatic contrast with the dark steel and reflective glass of the three modernist rectangular buildings of the Federal Plaza, designed by Mies van der Rohe. The public art scene in the Loop exploded during the late 1960s and 70s. Mayor Daley liked to describe the Loop as an "outdoor museum," and described Calder as "a truly great artist whose genius has brought so much delight to the world."

The summer of 2012 was one of Chicago's hottest, with temperatures during Fourth of July weekend reaching 103° F three days in a row. As a "heat island," Chicago experiences temperatures up to 10° F higher than nearby rural areas. In 1999, then-Mayor Richard M. Daley initiated the construction of a green roof on City Hall, in an effort to moderate the heat-island effect. The building's rooftop garden spreads out across over 20,000 square feet. It includes 20,000 plants of over 150 different species, mostly native to the Chicago area, selected for their ability to thrive in the hot, dry, and windy conditions on the rooftop. The green rooftop saves City Hall over $5,000 per year on utility costs. City Hall's green roof stands in stark contrast to the black tar and metal on surrounding downtown rooftops, but with 500 million square feet of green rooftops across the city, Chicago leads the country in green roof planting. The city offers sustainability grants to assist Chicagoans in both commercial and residential planting.

Pablo Picasso's untitled sculpture was met with some hysterics after its 1967 installation at the Chicago Civic Center (renamed the Daley Center in 1976 for the late Mayor Richard J. Daley, seven days after his death). Much of Chicago's public art at that time was part of the muralist movement, depicting social and political issues of the city's history. The Picasso sculpture, on the other hand, appears representative of nothing. Some members of the city council called for it to be exported to Paris and replaced with a statue of star Chicago Cub Ernie Banks. Public controversy was mostly about trying to figure out what it was. Children were overheard saying it looked like "a baboon with wings," "a lady," and "my little brother." Casual visitors probably didn't notice that the sculpture was cast out of the same kind of steel as the adjacent Civic Center building, nor could they know that its pieces were assembled in a nearby American steel factory in Gary, Indiana. Picasso never explained what it's supposed to be, nor did he accept any payment for the commissioned work, instead presenting it as a gift.

The dilapidated building originally on this site was the temporary home of City Hall after the Great Fire of 1871. The Rookery may have gotten its name from the "roosting" politicians or from its plentiful pigeon population, but in any case, the name stuck even after renowned architects Daniel Burnham and John Root designed a new structure for the site. Then they moved their offices in, where they made plans for the White City of the 1893 World's Columbian Exposition. Frank Lloyd Wright designed renovations for the building in 1905. Wright's renovation replaced much of Root's elaborate ornamentation with white marble, for a sleeker design. For example, while the structure and the decorative Arabic elements of Root's original staircase are intact, Wright imposed a more geometrical design and encased the original terracotta and ironwork in white marble. The Rookery Lobby is Wright's only downtown Chicago contribution to architectural design.

The Quincy Street Station is one of only a few original L stations left in the city. It was built in 1897 as part of the first section of elevated rail (the "L") that would revolutionize commuting for Chicagoans on all three sides – South, West, and North, in that order. This section of track, a rough circle bounded by Wabash, Van Buren, Wells, and Lake Streets, provided an enduring nickname for Chicago's downtown: "the Loop." Service was provided first to the South Side, and later the West Side, in half the time of streetcars. Increasing traffic congestion in the Loop – pedestrian and automobile – slowed down the streetcars even further, making it clear that Chicago's transportation needed to function on an entirely different level, literally. Chicago's streetcars endured even after the new Chicago Transit Authority, which ran the L system, bought out the Chicago Surface Line in 1948 and garaged its last streetcar 10 years later. Meanwhile, the elevated rail system continued expanding, adding new rails underground and connecting the Loop to Chicago's two major airports.

32

The Joffrey Ballet of Chicago started out as a touring company with its base in New York City, until it made Chicago its permanent home in 1995. The move makes sense, considering that the company's unique style is a departure from classical ballet. It arises out of the distinct perspectives of its two founders, Robert Joffrey and Gerald Arpino. Joffrey's exploration of new ways to put on classical works combined with Arpino's high-energy choreography and counterculture themes make for a distinctive, electrifying experience. The company was the first to rock the ballet world with its performance of *Astarte* in 1967, which featured a psychedelic light show and projected film images while performers danced to a score that was entirely electronic. From there, the company continued to push the boundaries of traditional style, partnering with a modern dance company to put on the first "crossover" ballet – *Little Deuce Coupe* – set entirely to music by the Beach Boys. With appearances on the cover of *Time* and on network television, the Joffrey has integrated this elite art form into a broader cultural context. Chicago seems the perfect setting for the edginess and adventure of the Joffrey Ballet.

The Ledge, Skydeck

Willis Tower, 233 S. Wacker Drive

Although Chicagoans are still coming to terms with the renaming of the Sears Tower as the Willis Tower, there is no reluctance in taking the ride to the 103rd floor. This is the location of one of Chicago's premier attractions, the Skydeck. Opened in 1974, the 1,353-foot high observation deck offered unparalleled views over the city. Today the highlight of any visit is a trip onto the Ledge, which opened in 2009. The Ledge's four glass boxes extend out 4.3 feet from the Skydeck in what is the eighth-tallest building in the world, and only surpassed in the Americas by the CN Tower in Toronto and the antennaes of One World Trade Center. On a clear day visitors can see 50 miles and four states. The inspiration for the Ledge came from hundreds of forehead prints visitors left behind on Skydeck windows every week. Architecture firm Skidmore, Owings and Merrill designed the Ledge with 1,500-pound glass panels. The fully enclosed glass boxes retract into the building, allowing easy access for cleaning and maintenance. Each box comprises three layers of half-inch thick glass laminated into one seamless unit. The low-iron, clear glass is fully tempered for durability and safety.

36

French Market

131 N. Clinton Street

Chicago's French Market is no knockoff. It has authentic French origins – or rather, Algerian – in the Bensidoun family, who has been operating French-style markets in the Chicago area since 1997. The concept is not new to Chicago. In fact, it's more of a throwback. Around the mid-1800s, the public market was the only place Chicagoans could purchase non-wholesale amounts of eggs, meat, or vegetables. Less than a century later, Jewel Food stores would begin the trend toward the massive chain supermarkets with ample parking space – catering to households with both an icebox and a car – that still dominate the retail food market in Chicago. However, recent "locavore" and "foodie" trends have made the public market concept a welcome addition to Chicagoans' retail food options. After eight years of planning, the French Market opened in 2009, in a long-unused space connected to Ogilvie Transportation Center, a hub for suburban commuters – and tons of foot traffic. The market offers quick to-go options as well as retail grocery options from local vendors for both suburban commuters as well as the growing residential population in the Loop.

The Chicago Theatre was the Loop's first movie venue and a model for the design of other motion-picture houses across the country. When it opened in 1921, its patrons were mostly well-to-do Chicagoans who appreciated the extravagant interiors at least as much as the newsreels, stage shows, and motion pictures they came to see. Opening night's feature was *A Sign on the Door,* starring Norma Talmadge. The theater enjoyed great success over the next several decades, featuring both motion pictures and live performances by the likes of Duke Ellington and Jack Benny. Like many other theater venues across the city, the Chicago Theatre suffered declining attendance after the 1950s, eventually closing in 1985. However, it reopened a year later, completely restored and boasting Frank Sinatra's name on the marquee as the headline performance on (re)opening night. Today, the Chicago Theatre features live concerts rather than motion pictures, with a range of performers that includes rock bands, comedians, country singers, and even poetry slams. The six-story iconic vertical sign and marquee – which were a later addition to the building – serve as an unofficial emblem of the city.

Marina City
State Street at the Chicago River

An upgrade to the old "living above the store" model, Marina City was designed with the purpose of counteracting the mass exodus of Chicagoans to the suburbs after World War II. Residents of this "city within a city" could walk to their jobs in the Loop and return home to a complex with its own restaurants and theaters, as well as a bowling alley, a pool, and an ice-skating rink. Architect Bertrand Goldberg's design turned the European plaza concept, literally, on its side, keeping the pedestrian level open and spacious, and making functional use of vertical space above and below for parking and services. He described the apartments on each floor as "petals" radiating from a core of solid concrete toward an expansive balcony. More than 3,000 Chicagoans applied for one of Marina City's 900 residential units, which opened in 1962 with monthly rents starting at $115. The apartments were converted to condominiums in the 1980s. Commercial areas of the complex declined nearly to bankruptcy until they were purchased by the House of Blues in 1998 and transformed into a concert space and a blues-themed hotel.

Visitors to the Bridgehouse witness the history of the Chicago River as they meander up and down a winding staircase through five floors of exhibits. In the city with the most moveable bridges in the world, the Bridgehouse allows visitors to witness the massive mechanical structures that allow the Michigan Avenue bridge to separate at its center and raise its sides almost vertical to allow river traffic to pass. On a carefully orchestrated schedule, bridges open approximately 40 times every year. The Michigan Avenue bridge was critical to the city's development, providing a portal to Chicago's north side. The four exterior sides of the Bridgehouse present bas-relief sculptures that commemorate critical moments in the city's history: Louis Jolliet and Father Marquette's arrival, the influx of early settlers, the massacre at Fort Dearborn, and the city's recovery after the Great Fire of 1871. Some early bridgetenders lived inside bridgehouses, and their job responsibilities sometimes included firefighting, policing, and saving the lives of those who fell (or jumped) from the bridge.

St. Patrick's Day Parade (Dyeing the River Green)

Michigan Avenue and Wacker Drive

By 1860, Chicago had the fourth largest Irish population of any American city, and this ethnic group continues to have a strong and unique presence across the city on both the North and South Sides. Perhaps the pervasiveness of Irish influence across Chicago explains why the entire city can come together around the annual dyeing of the Chicago River and the downtown St. Patrick's Day Parade. The dyeing of the river came about by a fortunate accident, when plumbers discovered in 1961 that their coveralls were turning green from the dye they used to detect leaks into the river. Ironically, in its original form the dye might be called "Protestant Orange." But when it mixes into the water, by some chemical reaction – or, some believe, the magical interference of a leprechaun – the dye transforms into a beautiful Irish green, a luminous contrast to the murky green color that characterizes the river during the rest of the year. The event takes place at 10 a.m. on the day of the downtown parade, which always begins at noon on the Saturday on or before St. Patrick's Day.

Museum of Broadcast Communications

360 N. State Street

Chicago's location between two coasts makes it ideal not only as a transportation hub but also as a center for broadcasting – at least of the archaic radio-variety. Four of Chicago's earliest radio stations have been in operation for almost one hundred years. WMAQ, WBBM, WGN, and WLS all hit the airwaves in the early 1920s, and though programming has changed often, they are still a major source of news and entertainment for Chicagoans. The city's Midwest location also made it critical for networks to manage programming across time zones, to ensure 18 full hours of programming – and the ad revenue necessary to sustain operations. The soap opera genre was born in Chicago, as an experiment to determine the value of providing daytime programming. Clearly, it worked. Chicago also became home for the production of daytime talk shows, bookended by innovators Phil Donahue in the early 1970s and Oprah Winfrey well into the 2000s – with the likes of Jenny Jones and Jerry Springer in between. This museum is one of only three in the country dedicated to broadcasting, filled with memorabilia and home to the National Radio Hall of Fame.

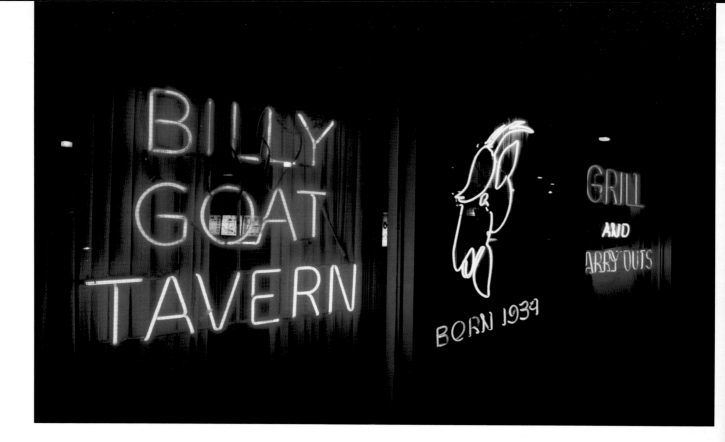

Long before Dan Ackroyd and John Belushi immortalized this legendary tavern in a recurring skit on *Saturday Night Live*, founder William "Billy" Sianis was himself a Chicago legend. In 1934 – a year after Prohibition was repealed – Sianis purchased the Lincoln Tavern on West Madison Avenue, near the Chicago Stadium (now United Center). He renamed it the Billy Goat Tavern after he adopted a goat that had wandered into the bar after falling off a transport truck. In his heavy Greek accent, he encouraged customers to "Try the double-cheez!" and offered "No fries. Cheeps!" Sianis is notorious for placing a curse on the Chicago Cubs during the 1945 World Series. Sianis purchased box-seat tickets for himself and Murphy (his goat) to attend Game 4 of the series against the Detroit Tigers. When Murphy was refused entry to Wrigley Field by Cubs' owner P.K. Wrigley, Sianis vowed that as long as the goat was denied, the Cubs would never win a World Series. So far, he's been right.

Garrett Popcorn Shops

Garrett Popcorn Shops have become a Chicago institution and gained an international following since they first opened at 10 West Madison Street in 1949. Family owned for more than 50 years, Garrett's popcorn has expanded its reach across Chicago and its suburbs, and across the country, and across the globe, as far as Dubai and Singapore. Popcorn has some history in Chicago, ever since Charles Cretors demonstrated his steam-powered popping machine at the World Columbian Exposition of 1893. Garrett didn't invent caramel corn — that was two other Chicagoans, German immigrants Louis & F.W. Rueckheim. But Claude and Gladys Garrett seem to have perfected the recipe to gourmet proportions, mixing it with their cheesy popcorn to create the famous trademarked "Chicago Mix." Garrett's popcorn is cited as a favorite of many famous Chicagoans — Oprah Winfrey selected it twice for her "Favorite Things" list, and First Lady Michelle Obama confessed to it as a "guilty pleasure" she enjoys in moderation. Garrett's still pops its popcorn fresh every day in hot air copper kettles before blending it with one of their secret family recipes, such as their latest — Smoky CheeseCorn. There are currently 11 Garrett Popcorn Shops in Chicago, including two at O'Hare International Airport.

"Gene" is Eugene Michelotti and "Georgetti" is Alfredo Federighi, who adopted the name of his favorite Italian cyclist when he opened a restaurant with Gene in 1941. A product of the American dream, Eugene emigrated from Italy when he was 15 – and spoke no English. He met "Georgetti" at the restaurant where he was a bartender and Georgetti was a chef. This arrangement worked well in their own place, where Georgetti became famous for his homemade ravioli while Gene worked the room in the front. Gene & Georgetti's has been family owned and operated ever since. The city's first steakhouse, it reflects Chicago character for more than just its meaty fare. In 1974, Eugene was indicted for attempting to bribe two policemen when they stopped him for speeding on North Avenue. Less than a month later, the indictment was quashed in the circuit court of a different judge. Frank Sinatra, Bob Hope, Russell Crowe, and Vince Vaughn are among the restaurant's swaggering celebrity patrons, but it is Gene & Georgetti's devoted following of 50 or so regulars that have allowed the restaurant to thrive in its original location for almost 75 years.

Holy Name is a cornerstone of the River North neighborhood, nestled among liquor stores and high-end restaurants, single-room-only bedsits and luxury hotels. Pope John Paul II celebrated mass here in 1979, and both Luciano Pavarotti and the Chicago Symphony Orchestra have performed at Holy Name. More notoriously, on October 11, 1926, a machine-gun shootout in front of the church left two mob bosses dead and five others wounded. A florist shop at 738 N. State was the headquarters for northside criminal operations, where boss Dion O'Banion had been gunned down by Capone's southside gang in 1924. In the pocket of one of the dead men that day, Earl "Hymie" Weiss, police found a list of jurists in the upcoming murder trial of Joe Saltis, a southside boss about to form an alliance with Weiss and drive Capone out of power. The origin of the gunfire that day was a second-story room at 740 N. State, one of two street-facing rooms on either side of the florist shop that were allegedly rented by members of Capone's crew. Saltis was acquitted a month later, but the steps of the cathedral were littered with bullet holes for years.

Chicago has a long poetic history, both for the rich subject matter it provides to poets and as a center for discussion, celebration, and publication. The Poetry Foundation itself, however, is a relative newcomer to Chicago's poetry scene. Its origin is *Poetry* magazine, founded in 1912 by Chicago poet Harriet Monroe, who also initiated the magazine's "Open Door" policy. Monroe wrote in Volume I, "May the great poet we are looking for never find it shut, or half shut, against his ample genius." Despite the masculine pronoun, roughly half of the first issue offered the "ample genius" of female poets. Since then, a new issue of *Poetry* magazine has come out every month, without interruption. In 2003, a $100 million gift from Ruth Lilly (philanthropist and heiress to the Eli-Lilly fortune) established the Poetry Foundation, allowing the magazine to remain independent as well as bring poetry to a wider audience, dispelling its reputation as an exclusive, elusive art form. It also gave *Poetry* its first permanent home. *Architectural Record* noted the building for its "economy of means and methods, just as a good poem employs an economy of language."

Water Tower and Pumping Station

821 N. Michigan Avenue

Before the construction of the Water Tower and Pumping Station, Chicagoans were accustomed to foul, muddy, even contaminated drinking water. The Water Tower and Pumping Station are a part of the waterworks constructed in 1866 to draw water from Lake Michigan, from a water crib two miles offshore. The 154-foot tower housed the standpipe for this system. William Boyington designed the structure with Joliet limestone in a style that has been called "naïve Gothic." On a visit to the city, Oscar Wilde called it "a castellated monstrosity with pepper boxes stuck all over it." Nevertheless, the Water Tower and Pumping Station is one of the city's best-loved monuments. One of only a handful of structures to survive the Great Fire of 1871, it became a symbol of the city's will to survive. The water tower has been obsolete since 1906, but it is meticulously preserved as a welcoming center for visitors, and beautifully lighted at night. The pumping station, though, carries on as a vital element of the city's waterworks.

In 1879, Samuel Mayo Nickerson, President of First National Bank, commissioned architects Burling and Whitehouse to build him a mansion. The Nickerson mansion would be the largest private residence in the city, and it would be fireproof. Builders used no wood on the home's exterior, earning it the nickname Marble Palace. Meticulous attention was paid to detail inside and out. For furniture, fixtures, carpets, and fabrics, designers recommended a mixture of styles, from Gothic and Renaissance to Byzantine and Japanese. Completed in 1883, the home appeared frequently in the news for Mrs. Nickerson's lavish receptions, as the couple continued to expand their collection of fine art and rare artifacts. In 1900, the Nickersons donated their entire collection to the Art Institute of Chicago and sold the home to businessman Lucius G. Fischer for $75,000. Fischer didn't touch the red leather walls, but he did have the magnificent glass dome installed. The home was donated to the American College of Surgeons in 1919, and purchased in 2003 by philanthropist Richard H. Driehaus, who set about a massive project to restore the mansion to its original Gilded Age magnificence, and then some.

This two-story restaurant/lounge opened in 1969 with the name "Sybaris," after those pleasure-seeking and luxury-loving Greeks (not to be confused with the couples-only Chicago-area motel chain of the same name). Under new management in 1993, it became the Signature Room at the 95th (and the Signature Lounge at the 96th). The experience is superlative in every way. The elevator ride straight to the 95th floor from the Chestnut Street entrance to the John Hancock Center may be the fastest in the city – 1,000 feet in 40 seconds. A seat in the Signature Room's east-facing dining room might afford the farthest views – across four states on a clear day – of any dining establishment in the city, as long as you don't count the slices of Giordano's pizza served at the Willis Tower Skydeck as "dining." The restaurant has received a myriad of superlative awards since its opening in 1993: Restaurant of the Year in 1996; one of *Gourmet* magazine's "America's Top Tables" every year since 1997; and "Most Romantic" and "Best View" in numerous local and national publications.

Several of Chicago's impractical Gilded-Age mansions have been converted into museums with some obscure, idiosyncratic focus. The one that houses the International Museum of Surgical Sciences was commissioned by the heiress to a match company – not the online kind but the striking kind. A relatively late addition to the mansion movement among Chicago's wealthy entrepreneurs, the building's architecture is straightforward Versailles. Its history is also straightforward, owned by the match-mogul Countiss family since it was built in 1917 until it was sold in 1950 to Dr. Max Thorek and the International College of Surgeons. The museum's regular collection consists of four main areas. Medical artifacts make up the largest of the four, including instruments dating back to an amputation saw with a reversible blade from the 1500s. Visitors can also view a collection of medical fine art, medical books from the 16th to the 18th centuries, and an extensive manuscript collection that includes letters written by Florence Nightingale. As well-curated as the better-known Mütter Museum of Medical Mysteries in Philadelphia, the International Museum of Surgical Sciences is only slightly less macabre and equally fascinating.

Very little of Lake Michigan's shoreline within the city limits is at its original level. Daniel Burnham's 1919 Plan of Chicago and the work of Parks Commissions in the 1930s brought about the eastward expansion of the shoreline. Much of the Lakefront Trail sits upon lake-bottom dredge, construction debris, wreckage from the Chicago Fire, and even rubbish collected from alleyways, all tightly packed and held in with protective structures of limestone, wood piles, and concrete. The trail offers almost 19 miles of pathway both north and south of downtown, with 50 access points along the way. On any given summer day, about 60,000–70,000 people use the trail for walking, biking, rollerblading, skateboarding, or training for the Chicago Marathon or the Shamrock Shuffle. The Navy Pier Flyover, slated for completion in 2018, will replace one of the most congested sections of the trail – where bikers and pedestrians currently share lower Lake Shore Drive with vehicle traffic. The Flyover will extend out from Navy Pier, to north of the Ohio Street Beach and south of the Chicago River Bridge, and be dedicated to bicycle and pedestrian traffic.

Chicago's North Avenue Beach and the original North Avenue Beach House are the result of a Works Progress Administration project. Roosevelt's New Deal provided $1.25 million to add massive amounts of landfill from North to Fullerton Avenues to create the 875,000 square feet of North Avenue Beach and construct a pedestrian overpass across Lake Shore Drive. The project also allowed for the construction of the North Avenue Beach House. The building was designed by Emanuel V. Buchsbaum, who made use of the then-contemporary art moderne style – think of it as the horizontal version of art deco. The style was perfect for creating the appearance of an ocean liner running parallel to the shore of Lake Michigan. The beach – and the beach house – were completed in July 1940. Six decades of lakefront exposure deteriorated the building beyond repair, and in 1999 Wheeler Kearns Architects designed a new structure, similar in design but larger, and made of concrete. Mayor Richard M. Daley dedicated the new building in May 2000. The roof of the beach house is a prime spot to watch the annual Chicago Air and Water Show.

In 1856, the Chicago Historical Society began as a group of businessmen interested in documenting the city's brisk and storied development. In a story of its own, the society lost its entire collection in the Great Chicago Fire of 1871. Undeterred, the society went about rebuilding. Also undeterred was Chicago candymaker Charles F. Gunther, rebuilding his caramel business after the fire while also adding to his massive collection of American memorabilia. After his death in 1920, the society bought his collection for $150,000, a purchase that established the society as a major historical museum and allowed for its world-renowned Abraham Lincoln collection – which includes Lincoln's deathbed and a towel stained with his blood. In 1932, the Chicago Historical Society moved into its new headquarters, a redbrick Georgian colonial in Lincoln Park. Building additions in the 1970s and 80s doubled its size, and renovations in 2006 transformed the Chicago Historical Society into the Chicago History Museum. The museum's annual Chicago History Bowl allows Chicagoans to submit ideas in competition for that year's special exhibition. "Chicago Authors" was the tournament's 2013 winner.

In a city wholly fabricated by street grids and orderly landscape design, the Nature Boardwalk at Lincoln Park Zoo attempts to return to some semblance of a natural ecosystem. Indeed, the South Pond around which it is constructed was entirely manmade, part of the original design of Lincoln Park. The South Pond was popular year-round, as an ice-skating spot in the winter and as a place to paddle around in a swan-shaped boat in warmer weather. But by the early 2000s, the pond had become a dangerous place to play, its asphalt walkway collapsing into water filled with garbage. In 2008, the city spent $12 million to transform the South Pond into an "urban ecosystem." The most notable feature of the Nature Boardwalk at Lincoln Park Zoo is probably the tortoise-shell pavilion, constructed of fiberglass pods held together by a frame of pre-fabricated bentwood. Although the entire Nature Boardwalk is designed as an educational experience, the pavilion functions as an outdoor classroom for schoolchildren and, occasionally, yogis.

Peggy Notebaert Nature Museum

2430 N. Cannon Drive

Twenty years after the Great Fire of 1871 destroyed their entire natural history collection, the Chicago Academy of Sciences was trying to recover. Their space in the Laflin Memorial Building (now Lincoln Park Zoo headquarters), consisted entirely of glass cases – children could look, but could definitely not touch. Eighty years later, the academy realized that the radical changes they envisioned would require a radically different building. So, they started from scratch, again. Heavy restrictions make building anything on the lakefront a radical undertaking. Architect Ralph Johnson's design could not rise higher than the treetops in Lincoln Park and its footprint could not extend beyond the buildings it was replacing. Johnson's design is a subtle reminder that the land beneath is man-made. The angular, cream-colored stone building suggests the shape of the sand dunes that occupied the site before it was packed with landfill to create more recreational space along the lakefront, while at the same time announcing the museum's progress into a new millennium. Taking nothing from the earlier location, the new museum opened in 1999 with interactive exhibits that children are encouraged to experience with all of their senses.

Second City

1616 N. Wells Street

New Yorker writer A.J. Liebling was no fan of Chicago, but he underestimated the resiliency of this great city, which took his derogatory moniker "The Second City" and embraced it. Today, rather than Liebling's scathing book-length attack on Chicago's arts, journalism, sports, and housing, the name "Second City" brings to mind the wildly successful theater company who appropriated the name. For over 50 years, Second City Theater has been entertaining Chicago. It not only set the stage for a new form of satirical comedy, it helped establish Chicago as a major theater venue and churned out talented alumni who brought their comedic gifts to international audiences. Perhaps its best-known alumni are the earliest cast members of *Saturday Night Live*, Dan Aykroyd, John Belushi, and Gilda Radner. This "second-rate" theater company went on to train the likes of Tina Fey, Steve Carell, and Stephen Colbert. The Second City Training Center offers classes in acting, improvisation, music, writing, and directing. Second City Theater currently has stages in Chicago, Toronto, and Los Angeles – but not New York.

Old Town Art Fair

1763 N. North Park Avenue

Old Town came to be known as such when, after World War II, community organizers formed the Old Town Triangle Association to maintain a sense of community in their growing neighborhood, founded mostly by German immigrants. This group has been running one of the city's most popular events, the annual Old Town Art Fair, for over 60 years. The event, which takes place on the second weekend of June each year, is considered the kickoff for Chicago's vibrant street-festival season. The first fair, held in 1950, was described as "a street art exhibit," and included everything from home craft projects to fine art. While the fair now includes mostly professional artists – many from beyond Chicago – it maintains its original mission to provide an independent venue for artists to exhibit their work and sell directly to the public. The event has expanded to include food vendors and a full weekend of musical performance, but the neighborhood vibe is evident in the many local residents who also open their patios to festival-goers. The Old Town Art Fair was named in 2011 as one of the country's top 10 art fairs by *AmericanStyle* magazine.

Old Town Ale House

At a time when the neighborhood tavern is a concept rather than a physical location, the Old Town Ale House remains true to its neighborhood roots – mostly. It was once the third and final point on the "Bermuda Triangle" of the North side – Riccardo Restaurant, O'Rourke's Pub, and the Old Town Ale House – the three-stop route of Chicago newspaper people on any given Friday night. The Ale House is still around, managing not to succumb to the recent wave of faux-authentic gastropubs replacing neighborhood taverns. In its second location – the first one across the street having burned down in 1971 – the walls are adorned with the original artwork of longtime regular, now part owner Bruce Elliott. Elliott's work includes portraits of former regulars like Mike Royko, Roger Ebert, and Nelson Algren, and his views on local and national politics are quite evident in his stylized portraits of Sarah Palin and disgraced former governor Rod Blagojevich. The tavern is still frequented by students and performers from nearby Second City Theater, still provides music via a jukebox, still doesn't serve food, and still only takes cash.

This mainstay tavern in Old Town operated as a saloon from 1890 until Prohibition – the constitutional amendment that paved the way for the huge success of Chicago gangsters – when it became Tante Lee "Soft" Drinks. You ordered your cocktails quietly in this speakeasy, and entered from the back. It opened as Twin Anchors, a rib joint, in 1932. The ribs are so tender, it's been said, that the bone falls off the meat rather than the other way around. One of the restaurant's most famous customers, Frank Sinatra, fell so in love with the ribs on his first visit in 1950 that he ordered them by air-freight when he couldn't make it to town. Frank also enjoyed the local intimacy of the place, always posting a bodyguard at the pay phone to stop overeager patrons from calling their friends to come see Ol' Blue Eyes in a rib bib. While Twin Anchors' menu has evolved to include a veggie "Soy"Natra sandwich and a gluten-free "Prohibition" barbeque sauce, the traditional "positively no dancing" policy is still strictly enforced.

The building that houses this quaint, street-level eatery is noteworthy in Chicago's mob history, but only by proximity. Across the street once stood the truck garage that was the site of Chicago's most iconic Prohibition-era gangland slayings on February 14, 1929, the St. Valentine's Day Massacre. And next door is the site of the lookout house. Here, members of the Purple Gang – Capone allies based in Detroit – watched the garage across the street waiting for Capone rival George "Bugs" Moran to arrive. The elegant building at 2121 North Clark had a slightly less dramatic history as the home of destitute families, murder victims, and streetcar-accident fatalities, before burning down in 1971. A year later, attorney Albert Beaver and contractor Charles Simital partnered up to restore the building to its original Italianate glory, including the pine paneling that lines the walls of the restaurant, which opened in 1973. Its signature pizza pot pie offers diners a unique spin on Chicago-style "deep dish" pizza – a flaky dough-bowl filled with cheese and sauce, with optional sausage and mushroom. Host Jesus Hernandez is known for creating a waiting list in his head by memorizing patron's faces.

Oz Park

2021 N. Burling St.

In the spring of 1967, a group of about 40 parents and their children marched at Webster and Larrabee to demand a new playground for their neighborhood, which at the time was rather dicey. They wanted the park named not for a dead president or an obscure war hero, but for someone children would recognize: Chicago author and creator of the Wizard of Oz, L. Frank Baum. In 1976 – when a new park was finally under construction – local bookstore owner John Lenhardt had even bigger ideas. He envisioned the park as a place of fantasy that children could step into by following a yellow brick road. "Children in a city need a sense of fantasy. There is enough stark reality living in a city," he said, as he collected 1,200 signatures in support of his idea. In 1988, hundreds of neighborhood volunteers constructed a playground of children's dreams – with winding walkways, rope bridges, tire swings, twin racing slides, and a life-size maze. Statues of the Tin Man, the Cowardly Lion, the Scarecrow, and Dorothy and Toto were all installed between 1995 and 2007.

Divvy Bikes

While organized cycling events like Bike the Drive – when Lake Shore Drive is closed to vehicle traffic – and the L.A.T.E. (Long After Twilight Ends) Ride have huge turnouts, the city's accommodations for everyday cyclists are a work in progress, though progressing much faster under Mayor Rahm Emanuel. In addition to increasing miles of protected bike lanes, the Chicago Department of Transportation also created Divvy, the city's bike-sharing system. Chicagoans can borrow one of Divvy's light-blue, heavy-duty bikes from any of the hundreds of Divvy stations across the city – open 24/7, 365 days a year. In its first weekend of operation, Divvy bikes were used for more than 4,000 trips. Divvy users can pay an annual fee of $75 or buy a day pass for $7. The light-blue bikes will begin sporting a Blue Cross Blue Shield of Illinois logo in 2014, as part of a sponsorship agreement between Chicago and the gargantuan healthcare insurer. And if Divvy bikes can resolve the tension between the cyclists who ignore red lights and the drivers who ignore bike lanes, Chicago may even break into the top 10 of America's bike-friendliest cities.

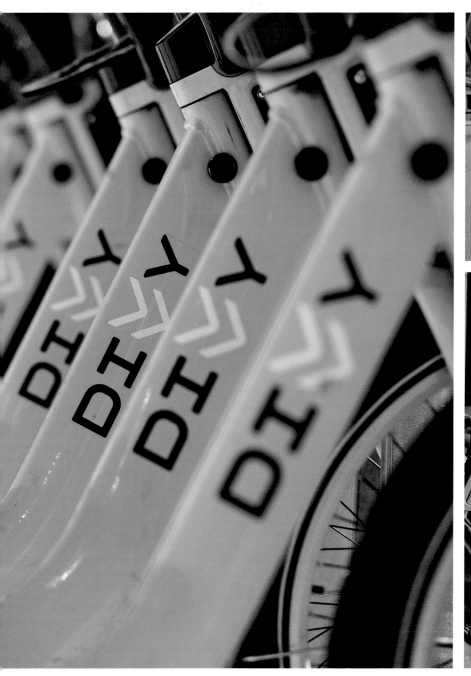

Shortly after the Music Box Theatre opened in August of 1929, it made headlines not for its avant-garde motion picture offerings but for the robbery of its box-office receipts. Assistant manager Clarence Balder was walking home after closing when robbers accosted him at Addison and Ashland. They took him back to the theater, where Balder surrendered $71 from the till. The bandits then, literally, twisted Balder's arm until he revealed that the rest of the money was at the home of theater manager Benjamin Lasker. At Lasker's home, the armed bandits again used their arm-twisting skills to force Lasker to admit that the rest of the evening's receipts – $957 – were stuffed in the couch. The building's architecture is not without a story of its own. One *Tribune* critic described it as "an eclectic melange of Italian, Spanish and Pardon-My-Fantasy put together with passion." The ceiling is dark blue with twinkling stars and moving clouds, lending an open-air atmosphere to the viewing experience. Today's moviegoers enjoy organist accompaniment to an eclectic offering of independent and foreign films, cult classics, and regular showings of *It's a Wonderful Life* during the holiday season.

By the 1880s, the saloon business was thriving, so the beer business would be, too, right? Not really. The Chicago beer market was oversaturated. Some larger brewers were even building their own saloons to ensure exclusive sales of their brand. Schlitz did this across the entire Midwest, having gained a following after shipping hundreds of barrels of beer to Chicago after the Great Fire of 1871. Schubas Tavern is one of the few remaining Schlitz saloons. In 1988, brothers Chris and Mike Schuba purchased the building, including the bar and the grill room – where, in pre-Prohibition days, women and children would hang out while their men drank up front – which had been remade into a small music venue. They restored the bar, inside and out, and they gave the grill room/music hall a makeover, which today is perhaps its greatest draw. Its modest back room offers fantastic acoustics to an intimate crowd seven nights a week. Well-known artists like Tori Amos, Bon Iver, Foster the People, the Shins, and Sufjan Stevens all made their Chicago debut at Schubas.

Wrigley Field is one of two prewar Major League ballparks remaining in the United States. Neighborhood property owners whose rooftops provide prime viewing access have a strong voice in the ballpark's operations – especially since they pay the Cubs' organization 17 percent of their rooftop revenue. The Cubs have not played in a World Series since 1945 and have not won a World Series since 1908. Still, fans are loyal and passionate, and continue to fill the seats day and night. In 2012, Cubs' owners proposed major renovations to transform the stadium into the sort of sports complex that traditionalists – and rooftop owners – fear most. Wrigley Field celebrated its 100th birthday in 2014 with owner Tom Ricketts' announcement that the family plans to go forward with the renovation on their own dime plus, of course, revenue from ads placed on the massive 4,000-foot video screen planned for left field, a screen that would obstruct the view from the rooftop decks across the street. A positive outcome for all negotiating parties – the Ricketts family, the rooftop organization, and the Mayor's office – is as likely as a 2014 World Series victory for the Chicago Cubs.

Prohibition didn't hinder the prosperous brewing industry in Chicago. By the time it was repealed, though, independent brewers could no longer compete with national brands. But Chicago's homemade spirit – literally – would not be down for long, not even in the midst of another economic crisis. When the Great Recession hit in 2007, Gabriel Magliaro was already well into the heady bureaucracy of producing and selling beer in the state of Illinois. Starting out with three employees and a contract with a distributor out of Wisconsin, Half Acre sold 800 barrels in 2007. In 2009, the brewery opened at its current Lincoln Avenue location, an upgrade from the spare bedroom in Colorado where Magliaro first began Half Acre's operations. Half Acre sells their beer in 16-ounce cans – the first brewer in Chicago to can instead of bottle – which can now be found on the shelves of the new Wal-Mart Neighborhood Market. But having been "picked up and carried on the shoulders of beer drinkers in Chicago," according to Magliaro, Half Acre remains a local brew in every way, expanding to a second location on Balmoral Avenue, a five-minute walk away.

Chicago's music scene is an eclectic blend of ethnicities and genres, all of which can be found at the Old Town School of Folk Music. Founded in 1957, when folk music was gaining popularity in city culture, the school is based on the folk conception as music for the common people. It offers group classes to amateurs who want to play music for themselves or their families or their communities – and the Old Town School has become a community in and of itself. Course offerings extend far beyond the guitar and banjo classes that were held at the school's first location in Old Town. Here, or at their newer main facility on Lincoln Avenue, students can take courses in everything from the accordion to the piano to the ukulele, as well as courses in theater and dance. The school also has a music store at 909 West Armitage Avenue (above). Events like Teen Open Mike and Six-String Socials offer students a chance to perform with each other and for the public. The school's Square Roots Festival is one of the most popular street festivals in Chicago's busy summer festival season.

Metropolitan Brewing

5121 N. Ravenswood Avenue

In 1847, Germans began to brew German-style – or lager – beer. German immigrants dominated Chicago's brewing industry for the rest of the century, supplying the lighter, colder lagers that the German and Irish immigrant working class wanted. Their methods also came to define brewing processes, as chemist and German immigrant Dr. John E. Siebel set up a chemical brewing laboratory on Belden Avenue, which would become the Siebel Institute of Technology, specializing in the brewing sciences. Many of Chicago's craft brewers today are graduates of the Siebel program, including Doug Hurst, who co-founded Metropolitan Brewing with his wife, Tracy, in 2007. Metropolitan Brewing specializes in German lagers, which require a four-week fermentation – twice that required for ales. These are the beers they prefer, although they do get creative, experimenting with herbs and produce from Green Acres Farm in Indiana. Their first special release blended their popular Flywheel lager with fresh mint and lime zest.

Graceland Cemetery

4001 N. Clark Street

Graceland Cemetery was built to replace the Chicago City Cemetery, which was closed in 1860 due to continuing fears of disease and water contamination. Worth noting is that the original cemetery's location – the current site of Lincoln Park – stood in the way of the city's northward development. Situated on 119 acres along Clark Street south of Montrose Avenue, the cemetery is distinctive for both the noteworthy – and notorious – Chicagoans buried there, as well as the architecture of its landscapes and monuments. Graceland is known as a "Cemetery of Architects" not only for these designs but also for the prominent Chicago architects buried there, including Daniel Burnham, Louis Sullivan, László Moholo-Nagy, Mies van der Rohe, and Richard Nickel – the young architectural photographer found dead in 1972 in a demolished Louis Sullivan building where he was salvaging artifacts. Monuments to captains of commerce Potter Palmer, George Pullman, and Marshall Field can be found among the lush grounds and winding roads of Graceland, as well as the more modest headstone of inventor Cyrus McCormick.

DANIEL HVDSON BVRNHAM
1846 — 1912
MARGARET SHERMAN BVRNHAM
1850 — 1945

Green Mill

4802 N. Broadway Avenue

Nightclub performers in Chicago's thriving music scene in the early 1900s were known for their improvisation, a method (or lack thereof) that infuses jazz with the energy and anticipation that appealed to its lively young audiences. Many of these clubs have come and gone, but the Green Mill has remained in continuous operation since 1907. Billie Holiday and Anita O'Day performed there early in what would turn out to be illustrious careers, and famous patrons included Al Capone and Frank Sinatra. Known for its combination of class and casual, the club suffered a decline in both after the Depression, and by the 1980s was known more for its disreputable clientele than its headlining performers. New ownership in 1986 began revitalizing the Green Mill with events such as Mark Smith's poetry slams and performances by Kurt Elling and Patricia Barber. Filled with memorabilia from its earliest days, this Chicago institution is enjoying renewed success. With the exception of the raucous Uptown Poetry Slam every Sunday night, patrons are asked (and expected) to be quiet during performances.

167	193
168 "SKYLINER"	194
CHARLIE BARNET	
169 "CHEROKEE"	195
170 "CHICAGO"	196
171 FRANK SINATRA	197
172 MA I TAHW AHleerely	198
173	199

Since opening in 1926, the Aragon Ballroom has met Chicago's shifting entertainment interests with varying success. Reputations of early dance halls as dens of iniquity were keeping the expanding middle classes away. The new Aragon Ballroom provided an air of respectability with strict dress codes and no-jazz and no-smoking policies. The club soon gained national acclaim, filling to capacity nearly every night. By the 1950s, though, social dancing was less popular, and attendance was in decline. During the next two decades, the club would be a skating rink, a boxing and wrestling arena, a psychedelic discothèque, and a monster rock-concert showground, where one tripping concertgoer "flew" from the second balcony and landed with a broken leg. The Aragon's offerings have lately been back in line with Chicago's diverse music scene, hosting artists in the 2000s as various as Ludacris, the Pixies, and Metallica. Every second Sunday during the summer, the Aragon also hosts the Vintage Bazaar, a pop-up flea market that caters to the thrift-store interests of the neighborhood's rising population of hipsters.

A passing fad in the mid-1960s, skateboarding enjoyed a renaissance about 10 years later that didn't stop. Skating continues to grow in popularity, on the streets, in parks, and as a professional sport. And for a Midwestern town like Chicago, streets are the only surf around. In the mid-1970s, even department stores were selling them. Chicago's Neiman Marcus sold what it called "the Rolls-Royce of skateboards," a clear-plastic model sporting the company's name, marketed for such upscale uses as "sending refreshments down a long bar, moving heavy plants, and practicing snow skiing." But skateboarding has always thrived outside of the mainstream, which may explain why privately owned skate parks never quite took hold in Chicago. Skaters tend to prefer public parks and the sidewalks – which are free. The Chicago Park District offers five skate park locations to skaters, including one in a viaduct beneath the Kennedy Expressway on Logan Boulevard. And while designer skateboards and gear are available from major retailers, most skateboarders prefer independent shops like Uprise in Wicker Park, which functions as both a shop and a cultural destination for skaters across the city and beyond.

The varied tenancy of Chicago's Flatiron building at the intersection of North, Milwaukee, and Damen Avenues in Wicker Park reflects the residential and commercial changes of the neighborhood. After World War II, the population was mostly working-class immigrants, blacks, and Latinos. The Flatiron Building housed a variety of small businesses, including a bakery, a realty management company, and various medical and dental offices and laboratories. By 1977 the building was vacant, as the neighborhood suffered further economic decline. The local Old Wicker Park Committee initiated an architectural rehabilitation project, planning to convert the Flatiron Building to Section 8 housing so the elderly could remain in the neighborhood when they could no longer afford the expected increase in property values. Over the next decade, local artists moved in, attracted by large, bright studio spaces and low rents. By the 1990s, these same artists could no longer afford their studio space as the neighborhood rapidly gentrified around them. Today, the Flatiron Building still operates as studio space for artists, but not so much of the struggling variety. Artists open their studios to the public the first Friday night of every month.

Logan Theatre

2646 N. Milwaukee Avenue

When the Logan Theatre reopened in 2012 after months of renovations, the line extended 500 feet down North Milwaukee Avenue. Opened in 1915 as the Paramount Theatre, this Logan Square fixture was owned by the Vaselopulos family since 1922. Chris Vaselopulos – rumored to have been born in the building – was highly active in the community, particularly in the 1960s after the construction of the Kennedy Expressway threatened the neighborhood's stability. He was a leader in the Logan Square Neighborhood Association, which is largely responsible for saving the neighborhood from further deterioration, demanding the enforcement of housing codes, decreasing shop vacancies on Milwaukee Avenue, and working with the CTA during construction of Blue Line to keep Milwaukee Avenue open. Inside the Logan Theatre, though, things fell into disrepair. Renovations after Mark Fishman purchased it in 2010 revealed the original art deco details, including marble walls and stained-glass transoms throughout the building. Spring-popping seats and sullied bathrooms were replaced, and a full bar was installed. The Logan Theatre has restored luxury and uniqueness to the moviegoing experience, as well as an independent spirit strong enough to rival any multiplex.

Fireside Bowl

2648 W. Fullerton Avenue

For decades Fireside Bowl was the busy host of leagues from all over the city and suburbs, offering 16 lanes and automatic pin spotters. By the 1990s, Fireside Bowl wasn't about bowling at all. From 1994 to 2004, Fireside Bowl was the place to hear DIY hardcore punk in Chicago. Sweaty mosh pits of up to 1,000 crammed into its 140-capacity space to see bands nobody had heard of, at least not yet. Alkaline Trio, Sleater-Kinney, and Fall Out Boy all performed at Fireside during its heady punk heyday. Faced with an eminent domain suit in 1999, owner Jim Lipinski stopped spending on repairs, thus amplifying the club's punk-rock aura. When the suit was dropped, he began renovating the space back into a bowling alley. Surprised patrons found out on August 21, 2004, that they were attending the Fireside's final show. They responded by throwing potatoes down the ball return. Fireside Bowl began hosting shows again in 2010, but it has not regained the following of its punk-rock glory years. Fireside's current web site highlights its "true Bowling Alley feel" as perfect for your next office party.

With Death Cab for Cutie headlining their 2014 annual Block Party, the Hideout is probably not really Chicago's best-kept secret anymore – although it maintains that atmosphere. There is no one kind of Hideout customer, except for the outsider spirit they share. The Hideout's 7-days-a-week show schedule brings together blue-collar, white-collar, and no collar for – depending on the night of the week – storytelling, comedy, writing slams, movies, poetry, kids' events and, of course, music. And through it all there is dancing. In 2009, the *Chicago Reader* voted the Hideout "the Best Place to Dance Your Ass Off." The bar is aptly named, even though the only sign identifying it as the Hideout is a hand-painted shingle hanging on a chain-link fence at the corner of Elston and Wabansia. Back roads and alleyways are the only route to the wood-frame cottage that looks like somebody's house, if it weren't for the Old Style sign above the door. In the age of the Internet, word-of-mouth advertising has taken on a whole new meaning, but it's the only kind of advertising the Hideout will use.

Michael Jordan Statue

United Center, 1901 W. Madison Street

The Chicago Bulls organization commissioned this statue to honor the legacy of record-breaking, world-famous – and then-retired – basketball player Michael Jordan. The bronze sculpture was unveiled at the official retirement of Jordan's #23 in November 1994, as his jersey was raised to the roof beams of Chicago's new United Center. The 11.5-foot statue captures the athlete's gravity-defying flight across the court, high above a cluster of blurry opponents, sporting a pair of his signature Air Jordan sneakers. Jordan's deal with Nike forbids the athlete from wearing any logo other than their signature swish, on his shoes or anywhere else. Controversy arose in 2010, when fans of Stanley Cup Champion Chicago Blackhawks – who share the stadium with the Bulls – dressed the statue in a Blackhawks jersey and skate blades, all adorned with the Reebok logo. The next day the logo was covered by Nike stickers, rumored to have been placed by Jordan himself, who covers the logo on his Blackhawks jersey when he attends their games. Incidentally, less than a year after the unveiling ceremony Jordan emerged from retirement to rejoin the Chicago Bulls.

Garfield Park Conservatory

100 N. Central Park Avenue

During the reform-minded city politics of the early 1900s, conservationist and landscape architect Jens Jensen was put in charge of revitalizing the city's green spaces. He rebuilt the Garfield Park Conservatory, employing Prairie-style design with low, simple structures with wide glass vistas for exhibiting and viewing plant life. This West Side neighborhood has suffered from the effects of the Depression, the displacement of its residents due to the construction of the Eisenhower Expressway, and the imposition of public housing projects. Garfield Park is a neighborhood with a history of community activism, including rent strikes and protests against absentee landlords. Massive riots after the assassination of Martin Luther King, Jr., destroyed much of the neighborhood and many residents fled. Still, the spirit of community activism prevails, and the conservatory is central to many of these efforts. In addition to educational programs from early childhood to university extension projects, the conservatory offers regular and special exhibits, including the work of artists such as glass sculptor Dale Chihuly. It has also become a popular venue for field trips and weddings.

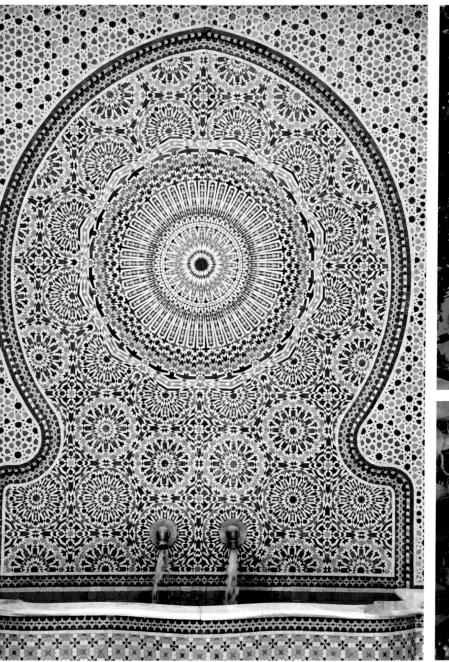
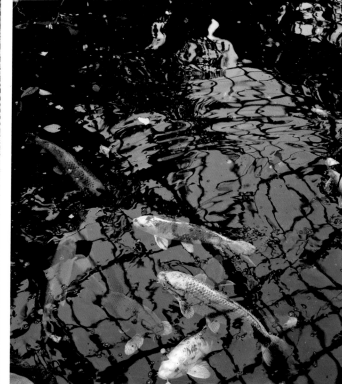

Hubbard Street Dance Chicago

1147 W. Jackson Boulevard

Hubbard Street in River North has always been an avenue for artistic expression among artists who exist outside the formal gallery scene. The street was the right location and the late 1970s was the right time for the Hubbard Street Dance Company. Broadway dancer Lou Conte opened the Lou Conte Dance Studio on Hubbard Street in 1972. In 1977, four women – the best of Conte's students – began performing locally as the Hubbard Street Dance Company. Modern dance was taking hold in Chicago, a city with a nontraditional arts scene where the eclectic styles of modern dance could find a home. The Hubbard Street Dance Company's four dancers grew to 11 in 1986, and was up to 20 in 1994. Today, the main company consists of 18 dancers. A second company, HS2, which consists of six dancers between the ages of 18 and 25, serves as a training ground for younger dancers and choreographers. Hubbard Street Dance Chicago is one of the only professional dance companies with a year-round touring schedule. The Lou Conte Dance Studio is now located within the Hubbard Street Dance Center on West Jackson Boulevard and offers classes and workshops for professional and aspiring dancers.

35YEARS

Nobody thought George Randazzo's dream of an Italian American Boxing Hall of Fame would ever become a reality, that his passion for boxing memorabilia was nothing more than a hobby. But George put his vision to the test when he organized a fund-raising dinner and invited living Italian American boxing greats of all weight classes – and the offspring of those who made boxing history. In September 1977, more than 2,500 people crammed into the Holiday Inn at O'Hare Airport to attend the Hall of Fame banquet – and paid $50 for the privilege. A year later, the banquet would honor Italian American baseball legends, basketball greats, and even jockeys. The Italian American Sports Hall of Fame was born, with the dual purpose of honoring Italian American athletes and raising money for scholarships and charity. Visitors can pay tribute to Hall-of-Famers such as racing legend Mario Andretti, bodybuilder Charles Atlas, figure skater Brian Boitano, and Chicago Cub Phil Cavarretta. They can also see the jersey of Lennie Merullo, the last living Cub to have played the beleaguered team's most recent World Series – in 1945.

Manny's Deli

1141 S. Jefferson Street

Original owner Jack Raskin's teenage son Emanuel was not the only inspiration for the name of what would become a Chicago institution. Jack bought a property on Roosevelt Road (formerly 12th Street) near Halsted Street that had been named Sunny's, so changing the sign to read Manny's meant purchasing only two new letters. Russian immigrant Jack and his brother Charlie opened their first diner nearby at Halsted and Van Buren Streets, in an area filled with thriving Jewish coffee shops and delicatessens. After World War II, Manny's Diner came into being when Jack split off to open his own shop, taking with him many of the old Jewish family recipes he had cooked up with Charlie. His teenage son Manny started as a cook and eventually took ownership, moving it to its current location in 1964. His son Ken has been in charge since a few years before Manny's death in 1983, and runs the restaurant in the spirit of friendliness and tradition established by his grandfather. This deli relic's rich history is documented by the news clippings that cover its walls.

The design of the Adler Planetarium is itself symbolic, its 12 sides representing the signs of the zodiac, each one adorned by its own bronze medallion sculpted in relief by Chicago artist Alfonso Iannelli. Sculptures around the building have both literal and symbolic significance. *America's Courtyard* (above), by Brazilian artists Denise Milan and Ary Perez, reflects the shape of our own spiral galaxy, the Milky Way. Four concentric arms spiral out from a central core of one marble stone divided into quarters, forming a central compass. The sculpture is an observatory in itself – the lines of the rising and setting sun at solstices can be traced along the axes of the central circle. On the north side of the building visitors will see Henry Moore's *Sundial* or *Man Enters the Cosmos* (opposite), also both a tool and a metaphor. The crescent and crossbeam, or gnomon, at the sundial's center create shadows that allow for the measurement of time. Moore also added a gold veneer to the bronze sculpture to celebrate the "golden years of astronomy," from 1930 – when the Adler was opened – to 1980, when the sculpture was installed. South of the planetarium is John David Mooney's *Spiral Galaxies* (right), inspired by Galileo's drawings and early photographs of our closest galaxies.

Stephan Balkenhol's Man with Fish

Shedd Aquarium, 1200 S. Lake Shore Drive

Stephan Balkenhol's *Man with Fish*, permanently installed at the Shedd Aquarium, made it onto *Travel + Leisure* magazine's World's Strangest Statue list in 2010. The 16-foot painted bronze sculpture stands southwest of the entrance to the Shedd, in a shallow reflecting pool among images of flora and fauna from the sea. It's a playful mosaic, although a bit less playful than when it functioned as a fountain. Indeed, how could a sculpture of a 16-foot man appearing to squeeze a spray of water out of a 16-foot fish be anything but playful? Still, children (of all ages) love *Man with Fish*. The piece is typical of Balkenhol's work, which often features ordinary-looking humans, often at disproportionate sizes, sometimes in an unusual proximity to a disproportionately sized animal. The largest indoor aquarium in the world, the Shedd is part of the city's Museum Campus, which also includes the Adler Planetarium and the Field Museum of Natural History. Each building bears the name of the department store executive who provided the funds.

Mural Art

Although gaining increased attention in recent years from artists and hipsters, Pilsen remains predominantly a neighborhood of Mexican immigrants, many of whom had been forced to relocate from the Near West Side to make way for the expansion of the Chicago campus of the University of Illinois. Nestled between 18th Street on the north and 26th street on the south, with Halsted Street its main north-south thoroughfare, Mexican culture is evident on every street and underpass in Pilsen, from the street vendors to the monuments and, especially, the murals. Following from the mural tradition of Mexican social activists such as Diego Rivera, murals continue to be an important outlet for the political and creative expression of cultural pride in Pilsen. A public art project initiated (and partially funded) by Alderman Danny Solis and the Chicago Urban Art Society has brought about more murals by both amateur and professional artists, depicting Mexican cultural icons such as Frida Kahlo and Cesar Chavez as well as symbolic political messages in support of the labor movement or in protest against the gentrification of the neighborhood.

Through immigration and labor recruitment, Mexican people have been a vital part of Chicago's population since the Mexican Revolution coincided with the city's rapid industrial growth in the 1910s. Like Chicago's other immigrant groups, Mexicans brought their culture with them to Chicago, and this influence can be seen on all three sides of the city. Despite persistent discrimination in housing and wages, Mexican immigrants to Chicago have established a strong presence in city culture, particularly in Pilsen, where Mexican art and culture flourishes in the street festivals, the neighborhood churches, and the public art. The richness and the power of Mexican art is captured in the National Museum of Mexican Art, founded in 1982 as a concept and becoming a permanent exhibition space in 1987. Since then the museum has expanded into a larger space, but still adheres to its definition of Mexican art and culture as *sin fronteras*, "without borders." The museum's collections include art and artifacts from centuries of Meso-American and Mexican culture, many of which are shared across the United States and Mexico. The museum is also a site for performance, education, and community activism.

Jobs in the lumber mills, garment shops, and other large factories established in this near Southwest neighborhood after the Great Fire of 1871 attracted immigrants from Eastern Europe, who started calling the neighborhood Pilsen. The name stuck even when an increase in jobs during World War I brought a wave of Mexican immigrants to the area, and the culture of the neighborhood is still heavy with Mexican influences. These immigrants share a history as part of Chicago's working class. The building was once a factory for a working-class staple: macaroni. By the 1950s, Chicago Macaroni was one of the largest producers in the city, despite their unfortunate history of false labeling of their salad dressing, violations of federal labor laws, and unsafe working conditions – resulting in violent machine-related deaths of at least two employees. Real-estate mogul Joseph Cacciatore purchased the building in the early 1980s, long before Pilsen became the new place for cheap studio space. Joseph's son Joey developed a vision for transforming the building into a market and studio space for designers from fashion to furniture to music.

Lacuna Artist Lofts

Rem Koolhaas's design for the 2003 McCormick Tribune Campus Center might be a striking visual contrast to Mies van der Rohe's austere Crown Hall. Philosophically, though, Koolhaas may be closer to the School of Architecture's founder than he appears. Koolhaas has taken the modernist architectural ideals of Mies's generation – innovative use of new materials and building technologies in a rapidly advancing society – and brought them into his own. The corrugated steel Koolhaas used for the 530-foot tube to muffle the noise of the L may contrast with the sleek lines Mies preferred, but both options exhibit the materials and technologies of their time. While the reflective glass of the Campus Center building is perhaps too subtle a tribute to the ideals of the school's founder, certainly the 20-foot glass portrait of Mies is not. Intersecting diagonal walkways are based on Koolhaas's three-month study of pedestrian traffic patterns on the campus, suggesting an organic order arising from within the community rather than inflicted upon it. Shaped by the material forces and the perceptible needs of its milieu, Koolhaas's design is truly modernist.

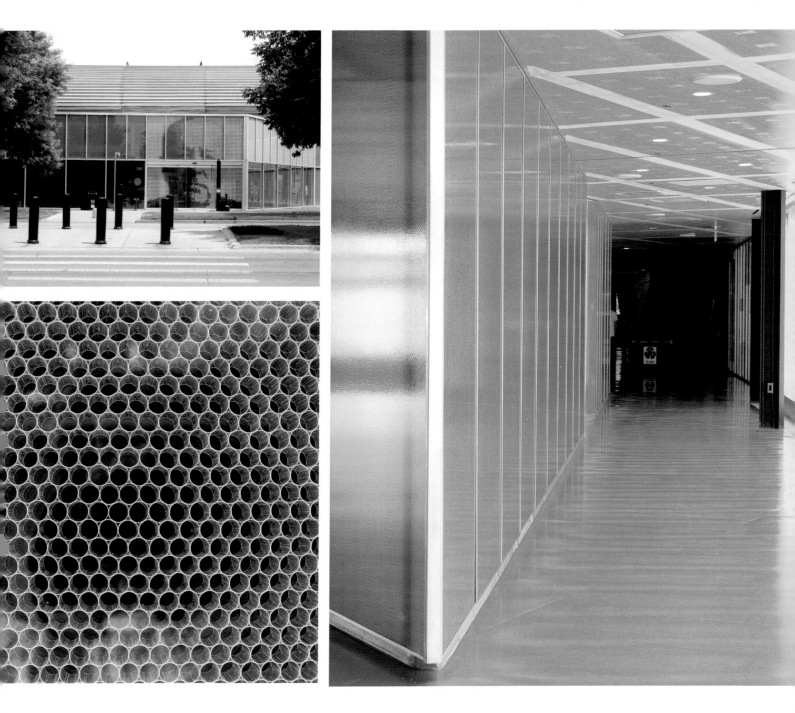

The McCormick Tribune Campus Center (MTCC)

Not a lot is known about Jean Baptiste Point du Sable, except for the fact that he was black (most likely Afro-French or Haitian) and that he sold some valuable property – including a large residence and a number of outbuildings – in 1800. In the empty historical spaces, a narrative has emerged of a fur trader living with his Potawatomi wife Catherine in a modest cabin along the Chicago River at Michigan Avenue. Besides a plaque on that site, the city's first permanent resident wasn't officially recognized outside of the African-American community until 1963, when Mayor Richard J. Daley finally agreed to proclaim the fourth week in August to be DuSable Week. Dr. Margaret Burroughs had already established the Ebony Museum of Negro History and Art in 1960, which evolved into the DuSable Museum of African-American History at its current location in Washington Park, a neighborhood with a long racial history of its own. An exhibit on gangs and gun violence includes a chain link fence covered in tags with the handwritten names of victims of violent crime (above).

After World War II, the Museum of Science and Industry became one of Chicago's most venerated attractions. Nothing captured people's attention more than the U-505, the German submarine captured on the high seas during the war. The man responsible for the capture, Captain (later Admiral) Daniel Gallery, was a Chicago native. He helped local business leaders acquire the U-boat from the U.S. Navy and arrange for its delivery through the St. Lawrence Seaway and all the Great Lakes to its new home in a special controlled exhibition site at the Museum of Science and Industry. A relatively recent addition to the museum's permanent exhibit space is the Crown Space Center, opened in 1986 in a new domed building with 31,000 square feet of space, including the five-story, 320-seat Omnimax Theater as a permanent attraction. The Omnimax's domed screen is over 70 feet in diameter, allowing viewers to be immersed in the projected world around them, which might be anywhere from within Mt. St. Helens volcano to the wilderness of Alaska, surrounded by a cloud of butterflies or inside a mother's womb.

Daniel Burnham's 1919 Plan of Chicago called for a "greenbelt," miles of lakefront public space devoted to cultural enrichment for residents and visitors. Burnham's original vision included a lagoon that would run parallel to the lakefront between Grant Park and Jackson Park. Northerly Island, at 12th Street, might have been the beginning of implementing this plan. Created by landfill, the island was meant to be one in a chain running south along the lakefront in order to create a site for water recreation. Although no more islands were built, let alone a lagoon constructed, Northerly Island marks the northern edge of Burnham Park (formerly Lake Front Park), and Promontory Point marks the south, at 55th Street. Designed by notable landscape architect Alfred Caldwell, Promontory Point's layers of native stone fit in with the Prairie aesthetic, as does the grassy meadow area dotted with trees around its perimeter. The spectacular view of the lake and the city's famous skyline from the south make Promontory Point a popular venue for weddings and other events, as well as an ideal place to view the city's Fourth of July fireworks display.

At 3:36 p.m. on December 2, 1942, three physicists under the direction of Enrico Fermi brought about the first nuclear chain reaction. It occurred at the University of Chicago campus – in an old squash court under the bleachers around Stagg Field – under the auspices of the Manhattan Project. In less than two years, the reaction they created there would speed up the end of World War II, when the United States dropped two atomic bombs on Japan. Henry Moore has been quoted, "It's a rather strange thing really but I'd already done the idea for this sculpture before Professor McNeill and his colleagues from the University of Chicago came to see me on Sunday morning to tell me about the whole proposition." *Nuclear Energy* was unveiled at 3:36 p.m. on December 2, 1967, 25 years to the minute that signaled the Atomic Age. Although Moore is known to have wished for viewers to circle the sculpture and peer through its open spaces, many visitors liken its shape to a human skull, or a mushroom cloud.

NUCLEAR ENERGY

HENRY MOORE – SCULPTOR

DEDICATED DECEMBER 2 1967

THE 25TH ANNIVERSARY OF THE
FIRST CONTROLLED GENERATION OF NUCLEAR POWER

AN EXPERIMENT BY ENRICO FERMI AND HIS COLLEAGUES

SITE OF FIRST SELF-SUSTAINING
NUCLEAR REACTION

REGISTERED NATIONAL
HISTORIC LANDMARK

THIS SCULPTURE WAS PROVIDED
BY THE TRUSTEES OF THE
B. F. FERGUSON
MONUMENT FUND

ON DECEMBER 2 1942
MAN ACHIEVED HERE
THE FIRST SELF-SUSTAINING CHAIN REACTION
AND THEREBY INITIATED THE
CONTROLLED RELEASE OF NUCLEAR ENERGY

The original site for this celebrated bookstore was the basement of the Chicago Theological Seminary in Hyde Park. In 1961, 17 book lovers anted up $10 each to start what would become a fixture of the community. The Co-Op now has more than 50,000 members, including Michelle and Barack Obama. The Seminary Co-Op has always been about books, the world of ideas and scholarly inquiry. Patrons and staff never seemed to mind the low ceilings and lack of windows (or coffee). By 1983, the Co-Op's success allowed them to open another location down the street, 57th Street Books, which offers a more generalized inventory but still functions under the member-owned model. In May 2013, the Seminary Co-Op had to move from its original basement location, after the building was purchased by the University. By contrast, its new home down the street is flooded by natural light coming in through the floor-to-ceiling windows. Patrons don't seem to mind this, either, as the spirit of intellectual discovery is still thriving. The historic bookshop and its recent move has inspired a documentary project led by two University of Chicago alumni.

Joseph Sapp, a farm kid from Ohio, started Rainbow Cone for exactly the reasons you might think: where he lived, chocolate and vanilla were the only options. As an adult, after his day job fixing Buicks, he and his wife, Katherine, founded Rainbow Cone on South Western Avenue in 1926. No plain vanilla, a Rainbow Cone layers chocolate, strawberry, "Palmer House" (vanilla with cherries and walnuts), pistachio, and orange sherbet, and in '26 would set you back 12 cents. The Spanish colonial-style Rainbow Cone building – an upgrade from Sapp's original ice-cream stand – topped with a flashing neon cone offers an old-timey carnival flair to your ice-cream experience. Closed during winter, Rainbow Cone's lines on summer evenings often extend around the block. But it moves fast – almost every customer orders the same thing, and scoopers are very quick with their paddles, serving up to 3,000 cones on any summer Sunday. The Beverly neighborhood on the South Side is one of the few left in the city where its mostly Catholic residents still identify by parish – Christ the King or St. Barnabas – although the castle on Longwood Drive that houses the Beverly Unitarian Church is a neighborhood landmark.

Michael Hayden's neon installation at O'Hare International Airport in Chicago – aptly titled *Sky's the Limit* – is the world's largest light sculpture. It consists of 466 neon tubes, which, if laid end to end, would create over a mile of neon light. It lines the long corridor that connects the United Airlines terminal to the rest of the airport, and travelers can gaze at it as they ride the moving walkways – as long as they mind the surreal feminine voice reminding them to look down. While these gentle warnings repeat themselves, the patterns of light never do. The dramatic piece was part of United's $500 million terminal, designed by Helmut Jahn in 1987, and meant to improve the ease of travel at the world's busiest airport. O'Hare International Airport is nestled within the city's near northwest suburbs. It stands on property that was annexed by the city in 1956 when it consolidated its airport operations, making for an unusual offshoot on a map of the city limits. Jahn described the experience of the terminal as "at once calm and peaceful, but at the same time adventurous."